Broken Heart, Healed Heart

By

Cynthia Spiers Sims

Table of Contents

Dedication i

Acknowledgments... ii

About the Author iii

Chapter 1 – Shame 3

Chapter 2 – Rebellion...5

Chapter 3 – Deception...7

Chapter 4 - Betrayal 9

Chapter 5 – Drugs 11

Chapter 6 - Incarceration..13

Chapter 7 - Disillusionment 16

Chapter 8 – Addiction 19

Chapter 9 - Denial 24

Chapter 10 - Broken Heart 28

Chapter 11 - Hope 32

Chapter 12 - Trials 38

Chapter 13 - Stress 45

Chapter 14 - Blessings 50

Chapter 15 – Reaping..54

Chapter 16 – Relapse 60

Chapter 17 – Uncertainty 65

Chapter 18 – Mistakes...69

Chapter 19 – Changes 71

Chapter 20 – Restoration...74

Chapter 21 – Healed Heart......................................77

Dedication

This book is dedicated to my two daughters, whose real names are not used to protect their identity.

Acknowledgments

Cover design by Jason Moehr

Moehr2offer@gmail.com

About the Author

Cynthia is a long-time resident of Tampa, Florida, originally from Picayune, Mississippi. She enjoys reading, writing, and loves to spend time at the beach. She is actively involved in her local church and serves in prison ministry.

Ezekiel 16:3-13

"This is what the Sovereign LORD says to Jerusalem: Your ancestry and birth were in the land of the Canaanites; your father was an Amorite and your mother a Hittite. [4]On the day you were born your cord was not cut, nor were you washed with water to make you clean, nor were you rubbed with salt or wrapped in cloths. [5]No one looked on you with pity or had compassion enough to do any of these things for you. Rather, you were thrown out into the open field, for on the day you were born you were despised.

[6] "Then I passed by and saw you kicking about in your blood, and as you lay there in your blood, I said to you 'Live!' [7]I made you grow like a plant of the field. You grew and developed and entered puberty. Your breasts had formed and your hair had grown, yet you were stark naked.

[8] "Later I passed by, and when I looked at you and saw that you were old enough for love, I spread the corner of my garment over you and covered your naked body. I gave you my solemn oath and entered into a covenant with you, declares the Sovereign LORD, and you became mine.

[9] "I bathed you with water and washed the blood from you, and put ointments on you. [10]I clothed you with an embroidered dress and put sandals of fine leather on you. I dressed you in fine linen and covered you with costly garments. [11]I adorned you with jewelry; I put bracelets on your arms and a necklace around your neck, [12]and I put a ring on your nose, earrings on your ears and a beautiful crown on your head. [13]So you were adorned with gold and silver; your clothes were of fine linen and costly fabric and

embroidered cloth. Your food was honey, olive oil and the finest flour. You became very beautiful, and rose to be a queen. [14]And your fame spread among the nations on account of your beauty, because the splendor I had given you made your beauty perfect," declares the Sovereign Lord.

Chapter 1 – Shame

Psalm 139:16 "Your eyes saw my unformed body; all the days ordained for me were written in your book before one of them came to be."

I believe the environment a child grows up in plays a significant role in shaping the life choices they make.   My upbringing wasn't the greatest, but it wasn't entirely my parents' fault, as you'll come to understand through my story.

I was born in Mississippi into a very poor family. There were four of us siblings: my oldest brother, Kent; my older sister, Cathy; my older brother Johnny; and me. The first house I remember was a white block home where we lived for the first eight years of my life. My mother struggled with mental health challenges, frequently experiencing nervous breakdowns that led to multiple hospitalizations. We had relatives in New Orleans, Louisiana - my grandparents, two aunts, two uncles, and my favorite cousin, Beverly, who was my age. Tragically, at age six, my grandfather molested both of us on multiple occasions, but fear kept me silent. This marked the beginning of my childhood trauma, profoundly influencing the choices I made later in life. My grandfather took his own life when I was ten, and a few years later my grandmother passed away.

During a visit to my uncle's home one year, my father left for a few days. Upon his return, he informed us that our house had burned down. Later, I discovered it was an intentional act to collect insurance money. We subsequently relocated to New Orleans. Eventually, we moved back to Mississippi and settled in the projects, relying on welfare benefits. Each school year, my mother obtained my clothes from the First Baptist Church. My father owned an old black Ford, and whenever we went out, I would crouch in the back seat to avoid being seen, already overwhelmed with deep-seated shame at such a young age.

At ten years old, my emotional scars deepened when I was molested again by two more family members. I became confused, ashamed and afraid. Were these terrible things somehow my fault?

It wasn't long before my dad started drinking heavily and often came home drunk. I hated those times, especially when he and my mom fought. They didn't just yell - they threw things at each other. Once, I even witnessed my mom cheating on him. It broke my heart because, despite everything, he was a hardworking man who tried his best to provide for our family. I loved my parents - they did the best they could with what little they had.

Chapter 2 – Rebellion

Proverbs 22:6 "Start children off on the way they should go, and even when they are old they will not turn from it."

We lived in the projects until I was 13 years old, then we moved to a house closer to the school I was attending. By this time, I was trying to live a Christian life despite my obstacles at home. I attended church regularly and had a best friend named Shannon. We were inseparable. She was the constant I needed in my life during that tumultuous time.

When I turned 14 and entered high school, I met a boy named Daniel. This marked the beginning of my rebellious years. Daniel had a car, which allowed us to spend time together, often outside of school. We started skipping school when I was in tenth grade, attending only two or three days a week. Over time, I lost interest in academics altogether. Eventually, we got caught and were suspended.

Despite my struggles, I always loved to write. English and literature were my favorite subjects. I spent hours crafting short stories and poetry. One of my poems, titled *"Why God?"*, expressed questions I had about my family life. I sent the poem to a local Christian newspaper, and it was published. Writing was my outlet, my way of processing emotions I couldn't talk to anyone about, especially my mother.

My mom often made remarks that opened the door for feelings of rejection to take root in my heart. I felt unwanted and unloved, which led me to bottle up my feelings and pour them into my writing instead. Our relationship was distant at best.

My family dynamics were complicated. My brother Johnny was always in trouble, frequently in and out of jail, until he was eventually sent to a detention center. In contrast, my older brother Kent was smart, talented, and a model student. He got good grades, played in the school band, went to college, and was eventually drafted into the Army. But he returned home and had changed after his time in the military.

Our home wasn't filled with warmth or laughter. Material things were scarce, and love seemed even harder to find. When I turned 15, I had the opportunity to leave. Little did I know, this decision would shake my teenage years to their very core.

Chapter 3 – Deception

Romans 16:18 "For such people not serving our Lord Christ, but their own appetites. By smooth talk and flattery they deceive the minds of naïve people."

This chapter contains sensitive issues, but it is an essential part of my story. Please understand that men called to preach, or any leader for that matter, are human. They are not immune to temptation, nor are they incapable of falling. As you read this, keep in mind that we all make mistakes. Thank God for His grace and mercy!

When I was in high school, I attended a small Baptist church. The pastor, Rick, was only 26 years old, married, and a father of three young children. I often babysat for them and occasionally spend the night at their house. Near the end of my sophomore year, Rick's wife, Joanne, underwent surgery and needed to rest for a few weeks after returning home. The family invited me to stay with them that summer to help with the kids, and I was eager to assist. I moved in as soon as school let out in June, thrilled to have my own bedroom for the first time. At home, I shared a double bed with my sister, so having privacy felt like a luxury. For the first few weeks, Joanne focused on recovery, and I managed the children.

One Saturday morning, Joanne left early to attend a business meeting two hours away. The kids were still asleep when Rick came into my bedroom—and we had a sexual encounter. I was only 15 years old. Tragically, it didn't end there. It continued for weeks, and each Sunday, Rick stood in the pulpit and preached. I was confused and deeply conflicted. Who could I tell? And even if I did, who would believe me? Eventually, Joanne found out. I was asked to leave, and

I called Daniel to come pick me up. Overwhelmed with shame and desperation, I decided to run away with him. We drove to Panama City Beach, Florida, and stayed there for a couple of weeks before returning home. I moved back in with my parents, but I felt like a shadow of myself.

Not long after, Daniel and I decided to get married. Ironically, Rick offered to officiate at the ceremony. He had one condition: I had to leave with him the following week. Blinded by confusion and seeking an escape, I agreed. While Daniel was at work, I packed my bags, left a note, and Rick picked me up. We drove to Baton Rouge, Louisiana and stayed there for three months. As Christmas approached, Rick announced he missed his children and wanted to go home. I was crushed. I felt discarded, like a used and forgotten item. He drove me back to my parents' house and that was the last time I had ever heard from him.

Amid this emotional storm, my parents separated. My dad moved out, and I tried to piece my life back together. A few days after I came home, Daniel visited. He forgave me for leaving him and asked if we could try again. Daniel's forgiveness and unconditional love mirrored the grace of our Heavenly Father. He and I moved in with his mother, and soon after, I became pregnant. While I was carrying our child, my father fell seriously ill. He was diagnosed with stage four lung cancer and given only a few months to live. One night, he stayed with Daniel and me, but the following day, he was hospitalized. A few days later, he passed away.

A month later, I gave birth to a precious nine-pound baby boy. We named him Charlie. At the time, I had no idea that my heart would soon be shattered again.

Chapter 4 - Betrayal

Psalm 34:18: "The Lord is close to the brokenhearted and saves those who are crushed in spirit."

After Charlie was born, I was overjoyed! He was a beautiful, healthy baby, and his arrival filled me with a renewed sense of purpose. When Charlie was just three months old, Daniel and I decided to move closer to my brother and his wife. We became active in their church community, yet despite these changes, I found myself unhappy in my marriage. This wasn't Daniel's fault - he did everything he could to make me happy. Still, over time, I came to the difficult realization that our relationship couldn't continue. After much consideration, I ended my marriage to Daniel, and Charlie and I moved in with my sister-in-law's family. Her sister Sarah, who was my age, quickly became my closest friend.

I'll never forget the night Sarah and I attended a church outreach on the beach. Daniel had kept Charlie for the weekend, and I'd told him where we would be on Sunday night, along with instructions to bring Charlie to the beach. I had already arranged for Sarah's mother to watch Charlie until I returned home. As dusk fell, Daniel arrived with our son. I asked him to take Charlie to Sarah's house, and he left without objection. But that was the last time I saw or heard from him. Heart-broken, I did everything I could to find out where he had gone. Eventually, I discovered he had taken Charlie to his father's house. I arranged for a court hearing; however, the judge ruled in Daniel's favor, granting him custody. Losing Charlie was devastating, and it marked the beginning of a dark and chaotic chapter in my life.

Through this journey, I learned the importance of self-worth and the strength that comes from trusting in God's plan. The heartbreak I endured became a catalyst for personal growth, shaping me into a more compassionate and determined individual. I realized that, even amid pain, there is hope for a brighter tomorrow.

Chapter 5 – Drugs

I Corinthians 15:33 "Do not be misled: Bad company corrupts good character."

I started working as a nursing assistant at a hospital and moved into my own apartment. It was a challenging but freeing time, and I soon found myself falling into a reckless lifestyle. I worked the evening shift, and after work, I often went to bars with some of the nurses. One night, while we were out, I met a man named Randy. We started spending time together, and my fragile heart quickly became attached to him. However, those feelings were one-sided - Randy didn't and never would feel the same. His true passion was drugs, not relationships. Randy introduced me to harder substances and eventually taught me how to use a needle. It wasn't long before my life began to unravel, and I lost my job at the hospital. I was caught stealing needles, a consequence of the dangerous path I had started to follow.

After a few months, I met someone who told me about a drug rehabilitation center in upstate New York. I decided to give it a try and stayed for four months. I even celebrated my 21st birthday while I was there. However, I wasn't ready to commit to the full year-long program, so I left before completing it.

Shortly after, I relapsed and found myself in the same destructive cycle. I reconnected with Randy, who was now living in Texas with his friend Paul. I took a trip to see him and what was meant to be a short visit turned into a stay that lasted a few months, dragging me deeper into the life I had tried to escape. Not long after, I discovered I was pregnant. When I told Randy, he was anything but supportive

- he wanted me to have an abortion. Reluctantly, I made an appointment at a clinic in Mexico, and Randy and I took a ferry across the border. However, we arrived late, and the clinic refused to see me. They asked me to reschedule, which I did, but on the way back to our place, I told Randy I had changed my mind. I couldn't go through with it. It was then I realized Randy had no intention of getting clean or changing his lifestyle. So, I left Texas and returned to Mississippi. My friend Sally kindly opened her home to me, and I gave birth to my second son and named him Anthony. Randy was absent from the hospital when Anthony was born, a stark reminder of the life I had left behind.

Randy eventually came back from Texas, and despite everything, we started seeing each other again. Together, we became involved in serious criminal activity. Randy began forging prescriptions, and I would take them into pharmacies to have them filled. We used some of the pills ourselves – injecting them - and sold the rest to fund trips to other doctors for more prescriptions. Soon we expanded beyond Mississippi, traveling to Alabama, Louisiana, and Arkansas to see different doctors. By this time, I was heavily using and became addicted. It was only by the grace of God that I managed to hold down a job and care for Anthony, even in the condition I was in. Somehow, I made it through the first six months of his life. But I was about to lose control entirely and set myself up for more heartbreak.

Chapter 6 - Incarceration

Ezra 7:26 "Whoever does not obey the law of your God and the law of the king must surely be punished by death, banishment, confiscation of property, or imprisonment."

Randy and I had a friend named Glen who lived in Louisiana and sold drugs. He was one of our main connections. One day we drove to visit him, and we had our six-month old son with us. It was our plan that I would visit a doctor and steal more prescription papers and then go to Glen's house afterwards. The first pharmacy we went to, there were cop cars surrounding the place. Then the police came out the front door with Glen, who was handcuffed. We proceeded anyway to another drug store to cash in the prescription. Randy told me to wait in the car, and he would take the prescription inside. Unbeknownst to Randy, the pharmacist suspected the prescription was forged and called the police. Randy and I went to jail and the Department of Children and Families were called to come and pick up my son.

I called my half-brother Kevin and asked if he would come to get Anthony. He and his wife came the next day and told the social worker that they would keep him till I got out of jail. After six weeks, I was released. I went to court and was placed on probation. I consented to Kevin and his wife adopting Anthony. I knew my son would be loved and would have a good life.

I started work as a waitress at a truck stop. When Randy came to visit, it wasn't long before I started shooting drugs again, as well as taking forged prescriptions to the pharmacy. One night I was working, and Randy picked me up when my shift ended. He had a prescription, and I took it into the pharmacy wearing my work uniform, which was stupid. While I was standing there, I saw the pharmacist get on the phone, so I ran out of the drug store, and Randy and I sped out of the parking lot before the police got there. Randy took me home and I went to work the next morning, as usual. I thought we had pulled that one off.

That day at work, a nicely dressed gentleman sat at my table, and I served him. I had no idea he was an undercover cop. He rented a hotel for us across the street. The next morning, we went down for breakfast in the hotel lobby before I had to leave for work. After we sat down, he got up and said he had to make a phone call. It wasn't long before another undercover cop came in the door and sat at my table. I was taken to jail, and I knew it was serious this time because I was already on probation. I was in jail for about three days, and my mom bailed me out.

Ironically, all during this time, I was still attending church. I had a court date set and my pastor's wife, Betty, went with me. I stood before the Judge for a second time and pleaded guilty to the charge. He told me he already had in his mind to sentence me to five years in prison. But because Betty was there to testify that I was trying to change my ways and get my life together, he sentenced me instead to a Christian rehab center for one year. I was there for the first phase of the program, which was three months. Then for the second and third phase, I was in Dover, Pennsylvania. It was beautiful in Pennsylvania, and I did well for the first couple of months. But I began to get restless and wanted to leave. The Director of the program bought me a bus ticket, and I went back to Louisiana. I moved in with my mom and stepdad and went back to work at the truck stop. Then

I became pregnant with my third child. Unsure of who the father was, I determined in my heart that I was going to keep this baby.

Chapter 7 - Disillusionment

Ephesians 5:6 "Let no one deceive you with empty words, for because of these things the wrath of God comes upon the sons of disobedient."

I was attending a small church in Louisiana when I met a man named Cliff. He was a single father with two sons and needed someone to care for them while he worked. I took the job, and over time, we became involved. However, I soon learned that Cliff was still married. His wife was living in Texas, though they had been separated for some time. Cliff eventually asked me to marry him, leading me to believe he was planning to start divorce procedures. Instead, he decided to move back to Texas to reconcile with his wife. Once again, I found myself heartbroken and disillusioned with the idea of love.

After Cliff left, I moved in with friends and stayed with them throughout the rest of my pregnancy. I had planned to deliver at a birth center located right next to the hospital, with a midwife overseeing. On a Friday morning, I went into labor and headed to the birth center alone. As the hours passed, the midwife became concerned when it was clear the baby was in a breech position. I had to be transferred to the hospital for delivery. That afternoon, around 5 p.m., I gave birth to my first daughter. Looking back, I can see God's hand in the situation. Shortly after my daughter was born, a nurse came in and said, "Now we are going to introduce your baby girl to Jesus," and she turned on worship music. In that moment, I realized that this was exactly where God intended my baby to be born.

After Grace was born, I stayed with my friends for a couple of months. However, I'll never forget what happened during that time. The pastor of my church asked me to leave, telling me I was like cancer to the body of Christ because of my promiscuous lifestyle. I believe they didn't know how to handle someone like me, but it still added to the hurt and rejection I was already feeling. After that incident, I stopped attending church altogether for a while.

Eventually, I heard about another small church and decided to visit. I enjoyed it and started attending regularly with my daughter, who was now two years old. I quickly became friends with the pastor, Timothy, and his wife, Brittany. They opened their home to us, and we lived with them for a time. During that period, I was able to focus on my education and earn my GED. Passing the exam and receiving my high school diploma was a proud moment for me – a small but significant step toward rebuilding my life.

Before long, things began to change. Pastor Timothy decided to convert the church into a mission for the homeless, which caused a drop in attendance, as a majority of members left. Undeterred, Pastor Timothy rented two vacant houses – one for men and one for women. I moved into the women's house, while Grace stayed with Pastor Timothy and Brittany. Being a house mom became my full-time job, and I loved it! For the first time in a long while, I felt like my life had real purpose. We lived and worked there for about a year, but sadly, the ministry never grew as we had hoped. Financial difficulties eventually forced us to shut down.

When the ministry ended, everything changed again. We moved to Jackson, Mississippi and became involved in another church. Timothy landed a job as a sales rep with a trucking company. But it wasn't long before I found myself caught in a web of lies and deceit that would shape the next chapter of my life.

Chapter 8 – Addiction

Galatians 5:1 "It is for freedom that Christ has set us free. Stand firm, then, and do not let yourselves be burdened again by a yoke of slavery."

In March 1986, Timothy, Brittany, Grace and I packed our belongings and moved from Jackson, Mississippi to Tampa, Florida. Initially, I continued working in the office while Timothy went on sales calls, and Brittany stayed home to care for Grace. It didn't take long before Brittany discovered Timothy and I were having an affair. When she found out, I moved out with Grace and got an apartment of my own. Timothy stayed with Brittany, but we continued seeing each other.

I quit my office job and started working as a server at a steakhouse. While there, I met another server, and we quickly became friends. Together, we started using cocaine. Through her, I met her drug dealer. Once I knew him, I didn't need to go through her anymore. And that only fueled my addiction further, and I started using more frequently. Even though Timothy and I weren't living together, he was still paying the rent for my apartment. That financial support enabled me to continue my habit, and I found myself shooting cocaine several times a week. When I started stealing money to fund my addiction, I finally admitted to myself that I was hooked. I'd even sneak into the bathroom during my shifts to inject drugs.

Once, while shooting cocaine, I missed the vein. The sore on my wrist festered into an infected abscess. Reluctantly, I went to the emergency room and admitted the truth to the doctor. He didn't sugarcoat it-my body was failing. He warned that if I didn't stop using drugs, I'd either overdose or end up in prison. His words frightened me, pushing me to check into a detox center. The detox program lasted only five days, just enough to stabilize me physically, but nowhere near enough for real recovery. During my stay, I was required to attend Narcotics Anonymous (NA) meetings every day. But five days wasn't enough to overcome the grip of addiction, and deep down, I knew the battle was far from over.

After I was released from detox, I returned to my apartment and was determined to stay clean this time. One night, there was a knock at my door. It was my drug dealer. He asked where I'd been. I told him I had been in detox. When he asked if I wanted anything and I said I didn't have the money, he pulled out a gram of cocaine, handed it to me and said, "Merry Christmas." That's all it took. Moments later, I was driving to the pharmacy to buy needles. In that instant, I ignored the ER doctor's warning and chose to stay on the same destructive path.

Eventually, Timothy and I broke up. I assume he stayed with his wife. I was too numb from the drugs to feel any kind of emotions. He faded out of my life, and honestly, I felt relieved.

As always, I turned to a new church for answers. One night, I flipped through the Yellow Pages searching for a church near my apartment. I called a number, expecting a recording, but a woman answered. It was Saturday night, and I had unknowingly dialed the pastor's home, where they were holding a Bible study. She told me about the church and gave me the service time for Sunday morning. The next day, I went. Despite looking like death warmed over - 90 pounds, with track marks on both arms and hands - I received a warm welcome. Everyone treated me with kindness. For the first time in a long while, I felt accepted.

Even though I kept using, I started attending this small church regularly. Pastor Barnett, his wife Claire, and another couple often came to the restaurant on Sundays after church. I knew they came to see me more than for the food, and that simple act of care meant the world to me. They never gave up on me. They prayed with me, discipled me, and poured their time into helping me grow. I'm so grateful for their love and patience. God even brought a spiritual mother into my life through that church – someone who mentored me and became the mother I'd never had.

I started dating a customer from the restaurant named Joey, and I got pregnant. When I told him, he immediately suggested an abortion and offered to pay for it, making it clear he didn't want the responsibility of a child. Looking back, I know the prayers from the people at church gave me the strength to see things clearly. I realized I had a choice: I could have an abortion and continue using drugs, or I could keep this baby and quit. For the first time in my life, I made a truly intelligent decision. I chose my baby. I informed Joey of my choice, told him I didn't want his money, and made it clear he would never meet this child. Then I ended things with him altogether. I shared with my doctor about my drug use, never imagining it could later be used against me.

I decided to pursue my education and enrolled in a vocational school to take a word processing course. During the day, I attended school, and in the evenings, I worked at the restaurant. Grace and I were living with a family from my church, and they were a tremendous help, caring for her while I worked.

I stayed in school throughout my pregnancy and that enabled me to become self-sufficient. With the federal grants and student loans I received, I was able to get my own place. For the first time, I opened a bank account and even bought my first car. Life was finally heading in a positive direction. At this stage of my life, I felt a sense of accomplishment and pride in the person I was becoming.

Two ladies in my church offered to be with me when it came time for my baby to be born. Labor began early on a Saturday morning, and Darlene, along with her husband, drove me to the hospital. Our other friend, Susan, met us there. Darlene and Susan stayed by my side throughout the entire day until I delivered. Because of my history of drug use, my doctor insisted on natural birth. At 5:58 p.m., she arrived. She was tiny - just six pounds and 19 inches long. From that moment, I've always called her my miracle baby. She gave me the reason I needed to leave my past behind and quit using drugs for good.

When Faith was born, the hospital staff contacted DCF due to my prior drug use. Although I had only used once during my pregnancy, they considered her to be high risk. I went home two days after she was born, and she stayed at the hospital. When DCF came to my house, they found everything in order - fit and ready for my baby girl to come home. That was the first of many calls that would be made to DCF. Faith finally came home on a Friday night, and I was fortunate to have the support of friends from church.

The first two years after Faith's birth went well. I returned to school and graduated in the summer of 1989. I can't describe the overwhelming sense of accomplishment I felt - It was the first thing I had ever completed in my life! Shortly after, I landed my first office job at an organization that housed the homeless, where I worked for four years. For a moment, it felt like everything was falling into place.

I wish I could end my story here, but this was only the beginning. I could never have imagined the heartache that I was about to face. The next two years would test me in ways that nearly broke me.

Chapter 9 - Denial

John 10:10 "The thief comes only to steal and kill and destroy; I have come that they may have life, and have it to the full."

I don't like to give the devil credit, that's not my intention, but he is real. The Bible says he prowls around like a roaring lion, looking for someone to devour (I Peter 5:8). And he knows our weaknesses. Mine has always been men. For two years after having Faith, I did my best to live a godly life. I wasn't dating, I was attending church regularly - not just attending but actively involved. Life was good. I was drug-free, focused on being a mom, and truly enjoying it.

Then I met Matt, the man who moved in next door. We started talking, and eventually he asked me out. I knew he wasn't a Christian. I knew I should have said no. But I didn't. We went on a date, and before long, we saw each other regularly. And just like before, I fell into the same pattern I could never seem to break. I became promiscuous again. It wasn't long until things quickly spiraled out of control. The consequences were devastating.

One Sunday at church Susan and her husband, Troy, approached me. They told me if I ever needed someone to take my daughters, they would be willing. Their offer was kind, but it felt unsettling – almost as if something unseen was already in motion. Pastor Barnett helped me to arrange a living will, granting them legal custody of my children should the need ever arise. I had the documents legalized and tucked them away in a safe place, never truly believing I would have to use them.

Faith attended the daycare at my job, and when I arrived to pick her up one Friday afternoon, I immediately sensed something was wrong. A DCF representative was sitting in the office with the daycare director, waiting for me. They asked me to step inside and then delivered a blow I never saw coming. They had reason to believe my daughter had been molested. I asked why they thought that, and the director explained that every time the staff took Faith to the bathroom, she screamed. She had also started becoming violent with the other children. These, they said, were clear signs of sexual abuse.

This time, DCF gave me an ultimatum. I had been reported twice in the last two years, and they made it clear that I needed to understand the gravity of the situation. The social worker asked about my boyfriend, and I admitted that we were seeing each other regularly. He was their prime suspect. She told me, in no uncertain terms, to get my daughters away from him immediately. If I didn't, DCF would take them into their custody. Panicked and desperate, I reached out to a friend, asking her to take both my daughters for a few days. I needed time to figure out what to do next – how to have Matt arrested for child abuse.

I arranged to have a detective come to my house when I knew Matt would be there. After dinner, the detective showed up and informed Matt that he would have to come downtown for a polygraph test. It's important to recognize that lie detector tests are not definitive indicators of truthfulness, especially in sensitive cases like child sexual abuse. Given the limitations of polygraph tests, it's crucial to consider other evidence and observations, when assessing such serious allegations. Faith's sudden behavioral changes are recognized indicators of potential sexual abuse. I felt torn and was in denial. However, prioritizing Faith's safety and well-being was paramount.

After this incident with DCF settled down, we moved out of the trailer and into a small two-bedroom house. That's when Matt started coming around more often - eventually he moved in. One day when my car broke down, my two daughters and I walked to the corner store. On the way back, Grace turned to me and said, "Mom, I don't want to be like you when I grow up." Her words hit me like a punch to the gut. I wish I could say that was the moment everything changed- that I turned my life around right then and there. But the truth is, my own selfish desires kept me trapped in the same lifestyle.

Not long after, I started having problems with Grace. One night, she stayed over at a friend's house next door. The next day, the friend's mother came over, upset - Grace had stolen money and cigarettes from her. I gave the money back, and when Grace got home from school, I spanked her with a leather belt. But she moved the wrong way, and the belt struck her back. The next day, bruises appeared. She showed them to her friend, who then told her mother. The woman called DCF. This was the third time DCF had been called on me. That Sunday, I came home from church to find police officers at my house. DCF was there with cameras. They took pictures of Grace's bruises and filed a police report. By some miracle, I wasn't arrested. Still, fear had settled deep inside me. I knew something had to change. I did love my daughters, the best way I knew how. And I wanted more for them. A better life, a different future.

I called Troy and Susan, and they agreed to keep the girls until the end of the school year. During the week, I talked to the girls on the phone, and on weekends, I saw them at church. I could see how happy they were. Being with two stable parents – people who could provide for them in ways I couldn't - made me feel like I was doing the right thing, even if it was only temporary. My plan was always to bring them home when school ended.

I thought I loved Matt. I believed we would get married. I was still chasing the dream of true love. But I kept smoking weed, kept living with Matt, and even started using cocaine again. I had relapsed. That relapse was enough to push me over the edge – enough to make me lose my children completely.

Chapter 10 - Broken Heart

Psalm 147:3 "He heals the brokenhearted and binds up their wounds."

One Sunday at church, Troy and Susan approached me. They told me they had been praying and felt the Lord was leading them to legally adopt my girls. I was stunned. That was a huge decision - one I couldn't make lightly. I told them I needed time to think and pray about it. It was the hardest decision of my life. Addiction had made me selfish, but for once, I wanted to make a choice that wasn't about me. I loved my daughters enough to do what was best for them, no matter how much it hurt. I wanted them to have a better chance at life than I ever did. And deep down, I knew Troy and Susan could give them that. So, I said yes to the adoption.

It was on a Saturday night after a prayer meeting at Pastor Barnett's home when I signed the papers. A few people were there as witnesses. I remember driving home afterward, tears streaming down my face. It felt like a part of me had died. Like I had failed completely. I sank into a deep depression, withdrawing from people. I kept asking myself, *"How did I get here?"* But the answers came easily – my selfishness, my addiction, my self-hatred, my lack of self-worth. All of it had led me to this moment, to the decision to give my children to another family. Grace was nine. Faith was three. And they were no longer mine.

Life moved on – at least as normal as it could for me. One thing that happened during that time was almost as hard as signing the papers. Pastor Barnett wanted us to have a ceremony where the girls, dressed in white, would walk down the aisle. He said it was for their sake, but I never fully understood the reason behind it. I didn't want to do it. To me, there was no point. The girls legally belonged to Troy and Susan. The deal was sealed. Nothing else needed to be done. But I was coerced into participating. And to this day, I can still see the scene in my mind, as vividly as if it were yesterday.

The piano music played softly as church members gathered, the atmosphere resembling a typical Sunday night service. But this night was different. The girls walked down the aisle, dressed in beautiful white dresses, each holding a bouquet of flowers. They took their seats on the front row beside their new parents. I had always sung solos in church, and I wanted to sing for this moment – one final offering. I chose *I Surrender All*. When I reached the third verse - *I give my all to Thee*, I changed the words. Instead, I sang *I give my girls to You*. As the words left my lips, I saw Grace on the front row, sobbing. Faith was too young to fully understand what was happening, but Grace did. And when I saw her crying, my heart shattered. I broke down and couldn't finish the song. I had to leave the stage. The rest of the night was a blur.

As if things couldn't get any worse, they did. Troy was in the Air Force, and I was informed that they were being transferred to Alaska. When they told me, I was devastated - but what could I do? They were the parents now. I was grateful I got to say goodbye to the girls on their last Sunday at church. Before they moved, I put together a scrapbook for each of them, filled with pictures and notes. I wanted them to have something to remember me by. Susan and I agreed it would be good for them. Still, knowing they were going so far away made the loss feel even more permanent.

I tried to adjust to life as a single woman without my children, but there was a huge, empty hole in my heart. Guilt and feelings of failure constantly weighed on me. How did I separate those feelings from my sense of who I was? I wasn't a bad person; I was just someone who made bad choices. Unfortunately, my children bore the brunt of those choices. I often wonder how adoption affected them. Did they feel rejected? Abandoned? Unloved? I never got answers. Once they arrived in Alaska, all contact was cut off. I couldn't call or write letters. Then I started hearing troubling reports from my Pastor about the girls. Grace was running away, and the police were bringing her home in the middle of the night. She seemed lost in a rebellious streak. I was told she had even threatened the family, and they had committed her to a mental hospital. Again, I was assuaged with guilt and was distressed that my former daughter was in a mental facility. In addition to all that, Pastor Barnett told me this was all my fault - that my lifestyle had caused all this. That I was costing the family thousands of dollars.

One year I shipped a box of Christmas gifts to the girls, and I included Troy and Susan's two other children as well. When I came home from work one day, I saw the box sitting on my carport, unopened. *Return to Sender* was written across the top. I was crushed. Heartbroken. I didn't understand. Was I going to be punished for the rest of my life for the mistakes I had made in the past? It certainly felt that way.

This was my turning point. I went inside and collapsed, weeping uncontrollably. I felt as if a knife had been driven through my heart. The pain was unbearable – indescribable. I did the only thing I could think to do - I turned to God. I cried out to Him, asking for help. I told Him I was tired – *tired of the pain, tired of the men, tired of the drugs*. They had taken everything from me. That's when I decided it was time for a change. I would start going back to church, and, once and for all, get Matt out of my life. I knew I had to make drastic changes before I ended up completely destitute and hopeless. I was already close to that point.

A girlfriend from church moved in with me, and I felt a desperate need to get away from the house I was living in. The memories of all the painful things that had happened there were too much to bear. We moved to a neighborhood nearby, and for the first few months, things seemed to be going well. My roommate and I were both working and attending church. We even got up early some days to attend the 5:30 a.m. prayer meeting at Pastor Barnett's house. But one morning, at one of these meetings, Pastor Barnett made a statement that shocked me. He implied my children would be better off if I was completely out of the picture. I can't fully explain how that made me feel. His words cut deep. That morning, I left feeling devastated and haunted by his cruel words. I started to wonder, *maybe he's right*. I even considered taking my own life. Today, I'm so thankful I didn't act upon that impulse.

Chapter 11 - Hope

Romans 15:13 "Now may the God of hope fill you with all joy and peace as you trust in him, so that you may overflow with hope by the power of the Holy Spirit."

For seven years, I had been part of this church, and during that time, it had been good for me. But after the adoption, everything changed. Joy felt out of reach, and I was constantly fending off accusations. I knew it was time to move on.

My neighbor, Brian, invited me to Grace Family Church. On the first Sunday of 1996, I decided to go with him. The moment I stepped inside, I knew this was the change I had been searching for. Brian and I became close friends, and I started attending regularly. Even after he stopped going, I continued.

When I first joined Grace Family Church, it was a small congregation of about 200 people meeting in a strip plaza. I loved everything about it - the people were genuine, the music was uplifting, and the messages were clear and relatable. Still, after spending seven years in my previous church, I wanted to be sure I was making the right move. I scheduled a meeting with Pastor Craig, and we met for lunch. He was kind and understanding, acknowledging that leaving a church after so long was like leaving a family. He encouraged me to pray about my decision.

During our conversation, I opened about my past – that I was a recovering drug addict and had placed my children for adoption. Before leaving, he mentioned he had another appointment and said he wanted to meet again. I knew in that moment that God was leading this decision. I had been seeking assurance, and Pastor Craig's willingness to invest time in me, with such unconditional love, felt so different from my past experiences with pastors. It was exactly what I needed.

Pastor Craig and I met again for lunch a couple weeks later and picked up on the conversation we last had regarding my decision to change churches. He said the church is like a hospital, that when you first come, you're a patient and must be treated to be healed. But there comes a time when you are no longer a patient, you get well and strong again, and it's time to get active. That helped a lot to clarify what I was already feeling in my heart about leaving my current church. I then finished with my story that led me to place my children for adoption. Afterwards, he said one thing that I will never forget, and it was a remark that changed the course of my life. He looked me in the eyes and said, "I believe you're free." WOW! No one had ever told me that before, that they believed in me. Not even my parents, and certainly not any of the men I had associated with. I left that restaurant feeling so encouraged and it was confirmation that I was in the right place.

I jumped right in and immediately became involved. I joined the choir and got involved in a small group Bible study. I found joy in giving and serving others. That's it – my joy was restored! Now I felt like I could put my past behind and finally focus on the future. My roommate moved out and I moved in with Pastor Craig's secretary.

Exactly four months after I started attending Grace Family, one Saturday morning my phone rang. It was my former Pastor, and he asked me if I wanted my children back. I was shocked! He said the girls were causing too much trouble and costing too much money and the family wanted to return them. I told him I would have to pray about it and that if I did get them back, things would have to be different. He told me I needed to decide soon.

When I hung up, I called Pastor Craig right away and told him about the phone call. I expressed my concerns and fears about being the mom the girls needed. He encouraged me to pray and if I decided yes, the church would help me. He suggested putting the girls in a Children's Home for a year and that would give me time to prepare to be a mom again. It sounded like a good plan and like something I could handle. But I still had to pray and be one hundred percent certain this was God's plan – not mine, not my former pastor, not Troy and Susan, not my new Pastor and his wife Debbie. This was totally between God and me.

I was reading my Bible during the time I was making my decision and turned to Jeremiah 31:15-17. "A voice was heard in Ramah, lamentation and bitter weeping, Rachel weeping for her children, refusing to be comforted for her children, because they are no more. Thus says the Lord: Restrain your voice from weeping and your eyes from tears; for your work shall be rewarded, says the Lord, and they shall come back from the land of the enemy. There is hope in your future, says the Lord, that your children shall come back to their own border." It only took a few days for me to search my heart and to know what God wanted me to do. Debbie was my greatest cheerleader. She told me she felt it was the right thing to do, and she also said she knew that I would be a good mom. She reassured me I wouldn't have to do this by myself.

I called Pastor Barnett with my answer, and he gave me Troy and Susan's phone number. When I spoke with Susan, we discussed when the girls would return, and she and Troy kindly offered to pay for the plane tickets. She also gave me the number to the hospital where Grace was staying so I could speak with her therapist.

When I spoke with the therapist, she was confident that Grace's behavior stemmed from missing me and simply wanting to come home. She assured me that Grace didn't have any mental health issues, just understandable emotional trauma from the adoption. After our conversation, Grace got on the phone, and she sounded so grown-up - she was 14 by then. I could tell from her voice that she was medicated. Our first call was brief, but we talked a couple more times before she came home.

We all agreed that the girls would come back, and we arranged their flight schedule, but there was one small hitch – the Children's Home had a waiting list, and it would be a few weeks before a spot opened. The next Sunday, before the girls were set to arrive, Debbie stood before the congregation and shared that a single mom who was new to the church was being reunited with her children but needed a temporary place for them to stay until the Children's Home could take them. Four families came forward that morning, offering to let the girls stay. Around the same time, a Bible study called "*Growing Kids God's Way*" was about to start. It felt clear to me that God was aligning everything perfectly for me to be reunited with my children.

The plane was scheduled to arrive on a Friday night. Debbie offered to go with me to the airport to pick them up. As we sat at a table waiting, I grew quiet. She noticed and asked what was wrong. Fighting back tears, I admitted I was nervous - I didn't know how the girls would react to seeing me again, whether they'd be happy or angry. Debbie listened patiently and reassured me that everything would be okay. She also suggested we visit her house the next morning so she could explain to the girls our plan for them to go into the Children's Home. Not long after, the flight arrived.

Debbie and I stood in the gate area, watching passengers come down the ramp, when I spotted the girls. As soon as they saw me, they both took off running! They wrapped their arms around my legs, hugging me tightly. It felt so natural, so right, like the years of separation had melted away in that moment. After gathering their luggage, we headed to the car. On the drive home, Debbie told them that we would be going to her house the next morning to talk.

Our first night together went well, though it's hard to explain the mix of emotions we were all feeling. Grace, still on medication, was quiet and withdrawn, while little Faith bounced around, full of excitement! The next morning while at Debbie's house, she asked the girls a few questions before explaining that they'd be staying with different families for a few weeks until space opened at the Children's Home. After the weekend, they would begin moving between homes. Sometimes the girls had to stay in separate homes due to space limitations, but the kindness of these families made a difficult situation a little easier.

One very special family took both girls in for three weeks, and during that time, they became like part of our own. Grace and Faith quickly started calling them Aunt Peggy and Uncle Pete – a name they still use to this day. I had never felt so much love from so many people at once. It was a beautiful lesson in selfless giving, a kind of love I hadn't fully understood until then. Eventually, we went to the Courthouse, where I stood in the judge's chambers and signed the papers to readopt them. It was a profound moment; one I'll never forget. To celebrate, we took a trip to Daytona Beach for the weekend. I didn't have a lot of money, but it was enough to rent a hotel for a couple of nights and enjoy the beach. It turned out to be a wonderful weekend – simple but filled with laughter and joy.

About six weeks later, it was time for the girls to move into the Children's Home. I drove them there, and it was an incredibly emotional moment - for me, and I'm sure for them as well. But I reminded myself that this was only for a year. Inside, I signed the necessary paperwork, then stayed with them while they settled into their rooms. Pastor Craig and my small group leader, Adam - who is also a dear friend - would visit them from time to time and check in to see how they were adjusting. Every weekend, the girls came home, and we used that time to reconnect. They seemed to be adjusting well to our new reality. At the Children's Home, they traveled to different churches to sing, and at Christmas, they were showered with gifts. The year passed quickly, but nothing could have prepared me for the challenges we would face when they came home permanently.

Chapter 12 - Trials

James 1:12 "Blessed is the one who preservers under trial because, having stood the test, that person will receive the crown of life that the Lord has promised to those who love him."

As the time drew closer for the girls to come home, it was time for me to move into my own place. I had been working as an assistant in a public relations office for almost a year, and I found an apartment close to my job. I took the master bedroom, while Grace and Faith shared a bedroom and bathroom. Grace and Faith came home in July 1997. I was ready to take on the challenge of being a single parent, confident that I could mother my children differently this time. I was a different person now, with a strong support system rallying around us. What I didn't realize was just how much I would need that support - because from the very beginning, things became much harder than I expected.

The first incident I remember happened one night when I came home around 9:00 p.m. I had left the girls at home, knowing I wouldn't be gone long. Before leaving, I made a pot of soup and left it on the stove for their dinner. When I walked in, the house was empty. The pot of soup sat untouched. Panic set in immediately. Where were they? Had something happened? I jumped in my car and drove around the neighborhood, searching for them, but there was no sign of them anywhere. My fear only grew. Desperate, I called Adam and asked him to pray with me. I was truly frightened. A few minutes after I got off the phone with Adam, the front door opened, and the girls walked in. Right away, I noticed something was off. Faith was behind Grace, carefully guiding her to sit down. I could sense it immediately - something wasn't right. "Grace, what's going on?" I asked. "I'm just tired," she mumbled. But I knew better. Her words were slurred, and it didn't take long to realize the truth - she had been drinking. While I was gone, she and Faith had visited a neighbor, and that neighbor had given alcohol to my 15-year-old daughter. I was furious!

Trying to stay calm, I told them to go to their room and get ready for bed. Then I called Adam to let him know the girls were home - and that Grace had come back drunk. While I was on the phone, a loud thud echoed from their room. My heart pounded as I hung up and rushed to see what had happened. There was vomit on the floor. Grace was slumped in the bathroom near the toilet, completely passed out. I helped Faith into bed, prayed with her and then left Grace where she was. She would have to sleep it off on the bathroom floor.

A couple of months after that incident, I lost my job. Not long after, my mom called with heartbreaking news - my brother Joey had passed away. He had been battling lung cancer, and though doctors removed one of his lungs, the disease had spread to his pancreas. Hospice cared for him in his final two months. I arranged for a friend to stay with the girls so I could attend his funeral in Oklahoma. I flew out and stayed with his girlfriend and her children for a few days before and after the service. Joey had lived a hard life, and he was only 43 when he died. But in his final days, he accepted the Lord while in Hospice care. That gave me comfort - I know he's in heaven.

After the funeral, I flew back home and soon received a phone call from Debbie. She wanted to meet with Grace and me after the Wednesday night service. That evening, I went to church while Grace rode with a friend - someone she had recently been introduced to. His name was Jonathan. When I met him, he and Grace both told me he was 18. When I walked into the meeting room, Jonathan was already there. The moment I saw him I had a sinking feeling that this conversation wasn't going to be easy. I sat down.

Debbie thanked me for coming and asked how things were going with the girls. I told her they were doing well and expressed how much I appreciated her support. Then she turned to Grace. "Grace has something to tell you," Debbie said gently. "She wanted me here when she told you." Grace's eyes filled with tears. Then, in a trembling voice, she said, "I'm pregnant." I felt like the air had been knocked out of me. This was the last thing I had ever expected - something I never imagined I would have to face. A wave of anger hit me, but I knew if I opened my mouth, I might say something I'd regret. Instead, I stood up and walked out of the room.

I remember driving around, tears streaming down my face. I was hurt, angry, and afraid. What were we going to do? I knew I had to calm down before talking with Grace. When I finally went home, the girls were already in bed. The next morning, as I drove Grace to school, I asked if she had a plan. She told me she wanted to stay in school and asked me to transfer her to a school specifically for unwed mothers. Other than that, she had no ideas or plans concerning the baby. After dropping her off, I went home and collapsed onto the sofa, sobbing. I prayed, asking the Lord what to do, how to handle this. It was bigger than me. I wasn't in a position - financially or otherwise - to help raise a child. I told the Lord I felt betrayed, and the moment I said it, He spoke to me: *"Daughter, I know how it feels – I was betrayed by many."* Peace flooded my heart and soul. At that moment, I knew – we would take it one step at a time, one day at a time.

One night, as I was coming home, I decided to return some DVDs before they were due. I left my purse in the car, thinking I'd only be gone for a minute. But when I came back, it was gone. Inside were all my IDs - my bank card, credit card, Social Security card, and some cash. My income tax refund had just been deposited, and I had at least $2,000 in my checking account. The worst part? My ATM PIN was in my purse. I returned the movies and rushed home to report all my cards stolen. When I called the bank, I found out $400 had already been withdrawn.

In just four months, I had faced four major crises. I truly felt like I was at my wit's end. Could anything else possibly happen? Unfortunately, yes. It could - and it did.

While at the Social Security office to replace my stolen card, I ran into one of Grace's classmates. We started talking, and I mentioned that Grace was pregnant and would be transferring to a different school. Then he told me Jonathan was 26 years old. I was stunned. I had no idea – I thought he was 18. After getting my replacement card, I went straight home and started making phone calls. I wanted to have Jonathan arrested. A police officer came to take a report, but when he finished, he told me there was nothing they could do. Since Grace had consented, her age didn't matter. I couldn't believe it. I felt helpless. The only option I had was to go to the courthouse and file a restraining order.

Grace attended the high school for unwed mothers for a short time before she and Jonathan decided to get married. It wasn't a fancy affair, but my dear friend Adam kindly offered to host the ceremony at his house. We kept it small, inviting only a few close friends, and some of Jonathan's family joined us as well. After the wedding, I told Grace and Jonathan they could stay with me until they could afford a place of their own. In September a beautiful baby girl was born, and they named her Sienna. Two months later, Grace and Jonathan moved into their own apartment, trying to build their life together. But a few months after that, Grace called me in distress. She and Jonathan had been fighting a lot, and she was scared. In their last argument, he had become aggressive and made threats. Without hesitation, I took Grace and Sienna to a safe place, where they stayed for a short time. Eventually, they came back to live with me. Now, we had to figure out the next steps.

We worked together to care for Sienna, but it quickly became clear that Grace wasn't prepared for parenthood - and I wasn't prepared to raise another child. When Sienna was eight months old, Grace made the difficult decision to let her live with her father, believing he could provide a better life than she could as a single teenage mother. I understood her choice completely - I had once made a similar one for my own children. But after Sienna left, Grace began to spiral. At 17, she got a job and moved out, determined to forge her own path.

After Grace left, I rarely heard from her, and I didn't see Sienna at all during that time. My career also became increasingly challenging. In 2000, I started at a new company, but by the end of 2001, I lost that position. After the 9-1-1 tragedy at the World Trade Center, the company downsized, and I was laid off.

Soon after, Grace started reaching out to me again. She had been living downtown and working at a restaurant when she met Tyler, the man who would later become my son-in-law. They moved in together, and in 2002, Grace became pregnant with her second child. Financially, they faced difficult times. After a few months, his parents stepped in and helped them secure a place of their own.

In January 2002, I started another job where I stayed for two years until the company was bought out. In just five years, I experienced two layoffs, and the last one left me out of work for eight long months. But despite the uncertainty, Faith and I never lacked anything. God was faithful, meeting our every need. The bills were always paid on time. A few times, I even received unexpected checks in the mail from my church. Having a support system during hard times is so important.

One Saturday night during a church service, I was sitting in the front row when Pastor Craig made a comment in his message. I responded with "Amen!" He must have heard me because he paused and said, "That 'Amen' means a lot coming from Cyndi, a single mom who lost her job." After the service as I was leaving, a couple standing near the back stopped me. "Are you Cyndi?" they asked. When I said yes, they handed me an envelope and simply said, "Merry Christmas." I thanked them but didn't open it until I got home. It was a check for $500. Once again, God provided in an unexpected but perfect way – right on time.

While interviewing for jobs, I refused to settle for anything that paid less than what I needed. I had offers but in faith turned them down, believing that God would provide the right opportunity – and He did.

During this time, my friend Stephanie, who worked at a law firm, mentioned her boss's husband was in the hospital and needed someone to sit with him for five hours a day. Since I was out of work, I took the position, which still allowed me the flexibility to go on job interviews. I cared for him for three months, but sadly, he passed away. However, God used this opportunity as a steppingstone to lead me into the legal field. After her husband's passing, his wife hired me as a temp at the law firm until I found a permanent job. While working there, I got a call from a legal placement agency asking me to come in for testing. I was nervous since I had no legal experience, but I took the online tests and passed – just enough to qualify for an interview in the very same building where I was already working. In 2005, I started my first legal job at a downtown law firm. It paid well, and I stayed there for seven years. God had given me exactly what I asked for because He knew I would need it for what was about to come in the years ahead.

Chapter 13 - Stress

Isaiah 41:10 "So do not fear, for I am with you; do not be dismayed, for I am your God. I will strengthen you and help you; I will uphold you with my righteous right hand."

In 2005, Grace gave birth to a beautiful baby girl. She was named Emma. Faith and I shared a two-bedroom apartment. She was 15 years old and in high school. That year marked the beginning of my struggles with her. She became friends with a girl downstairs, and they started spending a lot of time together. One night, Faith came home, clearly under the influence of something she had taken. I was furious – and helpless. I grounded her, but beyond that, all I could do was pray. I had never expected to face these kinds of challenges with her.

Around the same time, Tyler had left Grace with the two babies and gone to his sister's house, which was about an hour away. He left her without any way to care for the children. Grace left for Texas to spend some time with her half-brother Anthony, with whom she had been in touch over the years. This left Tyler to be the one to care for the children.

Tyler came back to their apartment with the kids, and I'll never forget the day I stopped by to check on them. It was heart-breaking. Dylon was sitting on the floor wearing only a diaper. Emma was in her crib, burning up with a fever. Tyler admitted he had no money for food or diapers. I went to the grocery store and bought some food, diapers and Tylenol for Emma's fever. My heart was so heavy, knowing they were trapped in this situation. The next day, feeling lost and desperate, I poured my heart into a long email to Debbie. I didn't know where to turn or how to help my grandchildren. Later, I learned the truth - Tyler had been smoking crack cocaine. That was the reason he had abandoned his family in the first place.

I met with Debbie to talk, and she suggested that I open my home to Grace and the kids. She said it was like God giving me a second chance to be a mother. I prayed about it and called Grace. She came back from Texas on a bus and a few days later, she and the kids moved in with me and Faith. Because we had a two-bedroom apartment, living quarters were cramped. Debbie told me the church would help me financially if I found a bigger place to move.

Shortly after Grace moved in, a small group from my church called "Redemptive Healing" was formed. I knew the two women leading it, so decided to join. It was a 10-week study, and at that time, I deeply needed the support of godly women as I navigated so many changes in my life. There were five of us in the group, along with the two leaders. The study was intense, but it brought profound healing to my heart, helping me process past wounds. It was during this time that I was finally able to forgive my mom. The Lord gave me a heart of compassion for her, allowing me to see her through His eyes. I also recalled something she had shared with me that had once hurt her. Understanding her past helped me make sense of her behavior and the struggles she faced with her mental health.

I rented a four-bedroom house just as my small group was ending in November. Grace started a job at a restaurant, working the evening shift. Faith came in from school and babysat Dylon and Emma until I got home. Faith came in as Grace was leaving. I relieved Faith when I came in, cooked dinner and got the children ready for bed. Faith became stressed during this time saying she didn't have time to do her homework and was getting behind in classes. I wanted to help Grace during this time, but it was hard.

At the beginning of 2006, I came in from work one evening and Faith was lying on the sofa and I could see she had been crying. After I picked up take-out for dinner, Faith did confess to me that she was pregnant and asked me if I would sign for an abortion. I told her no, knowing that I would be held accountable to God for that decision. We then discussed other options, and we both agreed that adoption was the best choice for her and the baby. I bought a desktop computer, and she took virtual online classes for school.

About one month later I was sitting in my bedroom when Faith entered and handed me a note. It was from Grace, who confessed she was pregnant by a man she worked with. Overwhelmed by the news, I knew I had to set a clear boundary. I told Grace that if she intended to keep this baby, she would need to move out. I simply couldn't manage two toddlers and a newborn on top of my work responsibilities. Grace ultimately decided that placing the baby for adoption was the best option. During this upheaval, I recognized my own need for support and began attending a group for single moms – a space where I could share my struggles and gain insight from others facing similar challenges. I also committed to one-on-one counseling, meeting weekly with two caring women for six weeks. It was through the grace of God, the strength of these support systems, and the unwavering encouragement from a dear friend that I managed to navigate this incredibly difficult time.

Faith and Grace both chose the same adoption agency - a Christian organization. They looked through profiles of potential families and were able to select the ones they wanted to adopt their babies. My dear friend Karla, who worked at a crisis pregnancy center, was a godsend to me during this time. She supported the girls throughout their pregnancies and offered me tremendous encouragement as I tried to cope with everything. I was especially grateful that the agency the girls chose paid all expenses. Faith had her daughter in September 2006 and one month later, Grace gave birth to her daughter.

Karla visited the hospital both times, offering her support. I had the opportunity to meet both sets of adoptive parents who came for the births. It was an incredibly painful experience for Faith and Grace - there were tears, deep sadness, and heartbreak. It was hard for me as well, knowing these were my grandbabies. I understand the pain of adoption on a personal level, having experienced it myself. I truly commend my daughters for the courageous choices they made. Each year they received pictures of their girls, which brought comfort and bittersweet emotions.

Life moved forward as best as it could, considering everything we had been through. When Faith turned 18, she moved into her own place. Grace enrolled her children in daycare, and I continued to care for them in the evenings after work. Then, one Friday night, I got the phone call all parents dread - Grace had been arrested for DUI, and the children were in the car with her. The police asked me to come pick them up, but I said I couldn't. That may sound like a selfish decision, but it was one of the hardest things I've ever had to do. I knew it was time to start letting Grace face the consequences of her actions. Dylon and Emma were placed in emergency foster care and eventually separated into two different homes. We weren't allowed to know where they were. Grace was granted supervised visitation at the DCF office. She was assigned a case worker and given a list of requirements she had to meet to regain custody of her children. They were in foster care for approximately a year and a half.

In 2007, I got a phone call from my mom with some difficult news – she needed open heart surgery. I took a couple of days off work and Grace and I drove to Mississippi the night before her operation. On the day of the surgery, my sister, my brother Kent, and his wife were all at the hospital with us. It was a long, emotionally exhausting day, but thankfully, she came through the surgery successfully. The hospital arranged for her to go to a rehab facility for recovery, and she did well throughout the entire process.

A few months later Grace completed all the court's requirements, and we were finally cleared to bring the children home. Since Grace was working, I made the trip on a Saturday to pick up Emma, who was now three years old. Later that afternoon, we went to get Dylon. It was an adjustment for all of us, but children are amazingly resilient. Each night I would sing to them, pray with them, and read bedtime stories. Before long, we had settled into a routine, and peace returned to our home.

Chapter 14 - Blessings

Philippians 4:19 "And my God will meet all your needs according to the riches of his glory in Christ Jesus."

The house we were living in had become a constant source of problems, and I didn't want to renew the lease. I wasn't happy with the landlord or the way we were being treated. In 2009, we moved into an apartment. I gave Grace the master bedroom since there were three of them, and it just made sense. Around that time, Grace made the decision to enroll in college to pursue a Paralegal degree. It was a good move for her. She attended school full-time, and the federal grants she received not only helped cover her education but also provided subsidized daycare for the children. It was a fresh start in many ways, and a step in the right direction for her future.

One Sunday at church, I was chatting with a friend when she mentioned a ministry she thought would be a great fit for me if I was interested. The ministry was called *Love's Way Out* at that time, and it served dancers working in strip clubs. I joined in 2007 and remained involved for 16 years. For our 15-year Anniversary, our leader renamed the ministry *Treasured Pearls* – a name that reflected the heart of what we were doing. Every third weekend of the month, we visited local clubs, bringing gift bags for the dancers. Each bag included our contact information and a small token of our unconditional love. Our message was simple: *You are loved, and you matter to God.* We never assumed their stories or judged their choices – we just showed up with compassion. Some of the women were single moms trying to make ends meet. Others were between jobs or waiting to return to school. Some didn't want to be there, and others had chosen that path. Over the years, we've seen many women leave the industry for various reasons. We've witnessed some truly miraculous things. I've had the privilege of mentoring a few of them, and I'm proud to say they're all doing well in their current life situations.

Several churches had stepped in to adopt clubs, offering intercessory prayer support and homemade baked goods. A couple of years after I joined, I was given the opportunity to personally adopt a new club for which we needed finances to provide additional gifts. God even placed a specific amount on my heart to give each month. I chose to be obedient, and from that point on, I faithfully gave every month. That step of obedience has stayed with me, and I learned that when I say yes to God, He moves in ways I can't always imagine – Ephesians 3:20.

At the time, I had been driving a very old, beat-up Honda that constantly needed mechanical work - and it needed a long overdue paint job. The repairs were becoming more expensive than the car was worth, and I was growing discouraged. I had been attending an intercessory prayer group that met weekly, and we had been praying for God to provide me with a better vehicle. One morning in January, not long after we had moved into the apartment, I received a call from a couple in our prayer group. They asked if they could stop by. They came in, chatted for a few minutes, met my family, and then handed me a gift bag. Inside was a set of car keys. I burst into tears because I had been so weighed down by the stress of my transportation situation, and this unexpected generosity overwhelmed me. They told me to come outside so I could see the car. Parked out front was a shiny red Chevrolet Alero. It looked like a sports car and, honestly, it was the nicest vehicle I had ever owned. Not only had they given me the car, but they also paid to have the tag and title transferred. The gas tank was full, it had just been washed, and they even provided a 90-day warranty in case repairs were needed. It was truly a gift from the Lord. God sees every step of faith, and He honors it in His own perfect way. My friends had no idea how God used their gift to build my self-esteem.

In February of 2009, on a Friday night, I received a phone call from my brother. Our mom had been taken to the hospital and was gravely ill. The doctors had given a grim prognosis, and Kent told me to be ready to come home if things got worse. At 4:00 a.m. the next morning, the phone rang again. It was the news I'd been bracing for - mom had passed away. It was Valentine's Day. I've always thought it was meaningful that He took her home on the day we associate with love. I drove to Mississippi for the funeral. Kent and I sang her favorite song. There weren't many people there - just a handful. One thing that has always troubled me is that I didn't cry. I loved my mom, but over the years I think I mostly felt pity for her. Deep down, I was relieved she was no longer suffering or living in poverty. It was a beautiful service, and I was thankful for the ones who came to show their respect.

In October, I was invited to attend a weekend retreat for women. It lasted from Thursday night to Sunday evening, and during that time, we had no access to cell phones or watches. The goal was to disconnect from the world and fully focus on Jesus. Over those three days, I experienced deep healing, and it was during that weekend that the love of God became real to me. Until then, it had always been something I knew in my head, but it had never truly reached my heart. Job 42:5 - *"I have heard of you by the hearing of the ear, but now my eye sees you."* That revelation changed my life. It brought me to a whole new level in my relationship with Jesus. I truly had a God encounter that weekend. The rest of that year passed uneventfully.

Chapter 15 – Reaping

II Corinthians 9:6 "Remember this: Whoever sows sparingly will also reap sparingly, and whoever sows generously will also reap generously."

The year 2010 approached - a year filled with even more blessings for us. One day at work I received an unexpected email from one of the counselors I had seen when my daughters were pregnant. She wrote to tell me that she wanted to give me her Toyota Avalon. You just can't out-give God! Now I had to decide what to do with the Alero I had been given just a year ago. I chose to give the Alero to Faith for her 21st birthday. It was such a blessing to bring her that kind of joy on her special day.

I had always wanted to go on a mission trip, and I had the opportunity to go with a team heading to Belize. I raised support from friends, and God provided every dollar I needed. We left in June for a seven-day trip, and it was an incredible experience. We ministered to inner-city children by washing their feet, giving them new shoes, and praying with them. Even their parents stood in line to receive shoes. We played games with the kids at the park, spent time at the beach creating artwork, and attended a Sunday morning church service. That service may have been the sweetest I've ever experienced. There was no music, yet the Presence of the Lord was unmistakable. The entire week was deeply humbling. I came away with a fresh understanding of how truly blessed I am. Everyday comforts I often take for granted - like clean water and electricity – are considered luxuries in Belize.

In September, a women's small group began at my church, and I committed to attending all twelve weeks. Each week, we watched a video that corresponded with the chapter we were reading, followed by a group discussion. As we neared the end of the semester, one of the chapters focused on material possessions and the importance of letting them go. During the discussion, I shared something that I had been carrying for a long time - embarrassment over my home. I felt ashamed to have people over because our furniture was old, torn, and mismatched - just like the home I grew up in. My daughter's bed sagged in the middle, and the dresser she used for her children had no drawers. I had never shopped for furniture; everything I owned had been given to me and had simply worn out over time. I didn't have the money to replace it, and that made me feel less than. But the message that night shifted my perspective. I realized that my worth isn't defined by what I own. It's rooted in God. That truth freed me from the shame I had carried for so long. At the end of the service, I shared my testimony – how the Lord released me from that shame and reminded me that my identity is found in Him, not my possessions.

A couple of days later, I received a message from one of the ladies who had been at the group the night I shared my testimony. Her name was Lianna, an interior designer, and she said she wanted to come by my apartment to give a couple of rooms a makeover. She arrived on a Sunday afternoon, walked through the apartment taking notes, and asked me thoughtful questions along the way. Lianna was incredibly kind and treated my family with the utmost respect. Before leaving, she said she would be in touch.

Just a few days later, I found out what Lianna really had in mind - and it was so much bigger than I ever expected. After seeing our apartment, she said she couldn't just spruce up a couple of rooms.

She wanted to give us a complete home makeover. She started making phone calls to friends and family, rallying support and planning for donations. The response was overwhelming.

I had no idea how huge this project would become. People from all over the world – many of whom didn't even know us - started donating. Some gave money, others donated furniture, and many gave a combination of their time, resources and generosity. Lianna asked me to make a list of what Emma and Dylon wanted for Christmas. She also told me that when the crew came to do the makeover, we wouldn't have to lift a finger - they would pack up all our belongings and move everything into the downstairs apartment we were transitioning into.

The weekend for our home makeover arrived, just three weeks before Christmas. Lianna had arranged for us to stay in a hotel while the crew worked. She told us to return to the apartment on Sunday at 4:00 p.m. To make the weekend even more special, she bought tickets to a nearby theme park, that included annual passes for all of us. We stayed at the hotel Friday and Saturday night, spending all day Saturday enjoying the park. Lianna also gave us plenty of cash to ensure we had a great time - and we did, especially Emma and Dylon. On Sunday afternoon, we checked out of the hotel and made our way to our newly made-over apartment. I truly had no idea what to expect.

When we drove up, there was not a parking space close to the apartment, so we had to park at the far end of the complex. A news team was there, along with our church's video team. Lined up on the stairs and at the front entrance were the special friends I had invited – people I really wanted to be part of this special moment. Pastor Craig and Debbie were there, along with our club ministry leader, my very special friend Karla, and of course, Lianna, her husband and their daughter. The video team from church even brought a yellow toy bus, and as we walked up, they started chanting, "Move that bus, move that bus!" - just like on the TV show *Extreme Home Makeover.* When Lianna opened the front door for us, I walked inside and immediately burst into tears. Everything was so beautiful!

The news team followed us as we went from room to room. The living room was decorated in a beautiful maroon color that matched the sofa and chair Pastor Craig had given us. A Christmas tree stood in the corner, loaded with presents underneath, and decorated with ornaments bearing the names of everyone who had contributed to our home makeover.

To the right, where the den used to be – the same space that once held the dresser with no drawers, they had created a bedroom for Grace. It was decorated in royal blue and black, with a white wicker bed and matching dresser that Debbie had donated. The dining room held a nice wooden table with four chairs, set with plates, placemats, glasses, silverware and a vase of flowers in the center. Two sheet cakes sat on the table; both decorated with the words *"Welcome Home"*. Against one wall stood a beautiful oak armoire. Next, we visited the main bathroom, where they had put in new towels, a fresh shower curtain, and coordinated decorations. Then we walked into the kids' room - which had been my old bedroom – and found two twin beds with brand-new comforters. Beside each bed was a brand-new bicycle, and a toy chest filled the closet, along with a dresser for their clothes.

Finally, we walked into the master bedroom. There was a new bed with a beautiful lavender comforter, a computer desk, and matching nightstands. In the bathroom, new towels were neatly hung, and a plaque on the wall read *Fairy Tales Do Come True.* It was in my bedroom that the news team interviewed me, capturing my emotional response to the home makeover on camera. When we returned to the living room, Lianna said they had one more surprise. She opened the center doors of a beautiful white entertainment center, revealing a brand-new flat-screen T.V. I had never owned a large-screen T.V. before. While we waited for the news team to return, Pastor Craig stated that since I had been a member of the church, I had become an example to all the single moms. Hearing that truly blessed my heart. When the news team came back in, I thanked everyone for being there and how much this makeover meant to me and my family. Channel 28 aired the story on the evening news and again the next morning. Even the apartment manager, who attended our big reveal, said our apartment looked better than the model unit they showed to potential residents.

One of the coolest things about this home makeover blessing was that it didn't just bless my family – it helped restore a broken relationship in Lianna's family. When she sent out the email blast about the home makeover, she included them, and to her surprise, they responded. They came to visit for Christmas, and Lianna's daughter met her grandfather for the very first time. It was even more special to realize that Lianna and her husband were the same couple who had blessed me with that $500 check six years earlier.

That Christmas was one of the best holidays we had ever experienced. It was so much fun to watch Grace and the kids open their gifts on Christmas morning - and there were even presents under the tree for me. In January 2011, during the second week of services, my church played the video of our home makeover, which included testimonies from Lianna and me. I think many hearts were touched that weekend.

It seems that right after every blessing, the devil tries to come in and cause chaos - and that's exactly what happened next.

Chapter 16 – Relapse

Romans 6:6 "For we know that our old self was crucified with him so that the body ruled by sin might be done away with, that we should no longer be slaves to sin."

Things became difficult that year. After taking a couple of years off, I rejoined the choir at church. That's where I met Alan, a fellow choir member. One Sunday after service, he walked me to my car and asked for my phone number. Before long, we were talking more frequently on the phone, then started going out to eat and spending time at the beach. The more I got to know him, the more I enjoyed his company. From the beginning, Alan made it clear that we weren't dating - he just wanted to be friends. I had been celibate for 16 years and was proud of that commitment. My intentions with Alan were purely to be a friend, and I believed if God wanted something more for us, it would unfold in His time. At times, we would pray together and read the Bible. My heart was truly in the right place when I met him.

The more time Alan and I spent together, the more comfortable we became in our friendship. But over time, I began to see a different side of him - one I hadn't noticed at first. He began cursing around me and wanted to go to bars. I realized I wanted more from Alan than he could ever give, and in that frustration, I threw all caution to the wind. Instead of pulling away from those feelings, I tried to meet him on his terms. I joined a weight loss clinic, started working out at the gym and began to dress provocatively. On the surface I felt proud - my body was changing, my confidence growing. But deep down, I carried a gnawing guilt. I knew I was doing it all to catch Alan's eye, desperate to break down the wall of "just friends" he had built between us. For eight months we spent countless evenings together. Yet despite our closeness, nothing changed. Not once did he cross the line I silently yearned for. Each time I dared to hope for something more, I was met with the quiet ache of rejection. It felt like a silent spiritual battle within me: a clash between the person I thought I should be and the woman I had become, chasing a love that could never be mine.

Eventually, I gave in to temptation with Alan. I continued to see him, and we were together for the next year and a half. Even though I knew he didn't feel the same way, my feelings for him kept growing. I became emotionally attached, convincing myself that he was meeting my needs. But then the enemy began whispering lies: *See what you've been missing all these years?* The more I listened, the more entangled I became – attached to Alan in ways that made me feel stuck and confused. He had always been honest about not wanting a committed relationship, but it still broke my heart.

In November, I was called into a meeting with Human Resources and was informed that my position was being eliminated. Due to a company restructure, my department was being merged with another, and my role was no longer needed. It was difficult news to hear, especially after spending seven years with the law firm. But even in that moment, God's grace was evident. They gave me six months' notice and allowed me time off for interviews, which gave me the space to search for the right opportunity without pressure.

One day at work, everything hit me at once. I had a complete meltdown and had to leave for the day. I cried out to God in total desperation. I felt trapped and didn't know how to get out - but I knew I had to, or I would lose myself. And God heard me. Alan received a job offer from a friend and moved out of state. When he left, I felt an enormous sense of relief. But I didn't realize just how hard it would be to rebuild my relationship with God. The damage ran deep, and it took time, commitment, and His grace to restore what I had lost. It was a long road – but I was determined to find my way back.

In 2011, I bought my first home. After six years, it felt good to live on my own again. I spent my first Christmas there, decorating a tree with ornaments signed by everyone who had been part of my home makeover. All the kids came over, and it was wonderful to be together and enjoy a delicious Christmas dinner.

I continued to look for another job, knowing my time at the firm was coming to an end. I had been informed that my last day would be July 3rd, 2012. I went on many interviews, but by the time that day arrived, I still hadn't found a new position. The girls I worked with were incredibly kind – they gave me a going-away card with money inside. I knew I was really going to miss this group of friends I had built relationships with over the years.

I found a great job after one week of my layoff. After everything I had been through - and all the time I had spent away from the Lord - I didn't feel like I deserved this blessing. But it was a perfect example of God's unconditional love and mercy. No matter what I had done or how far I had strayed, God was always there, waiting with open arms for me to return to Him.

I started my new job at the end of July 2012. But later that year, I relapsed. I was introduced to someone who was selling drugs, and I began using. This marked yet another downward spiral in my life. You see, Satan knows the call God has placed on my life. First, he tried to use a man to pull me away from my relationship with God. Now he was coming at me from a different angle - through drugs, something I had been free of for years. I used for about eight months before I even realized I was addicted again.

The year 2013 arrived, and it turned out to be one of the hardest years I ever had to endure. One morning, as I was getting ready for work, my phone rang. It was Faith's boss's wife telling me Faith had been in a car accident and was in the emergency room. I immediately called into work and rushed to the hospital. When I arrived, Faith was still in the ER, and I was able to speak with the doctor treating her. She had a broken arm and several bruises, but the doctor said she was incredibly lucky. After seeing photos of the car she was driving, I agreed - it was a miracle she had survived. She eventually needed surgery on her arm. The recovery was slow and painful, but I did everything I could to help her through it.

In addition to dealing with the stress I was already feeling from Faith's accident, things at work began to spiral. In September, I was called into my boss's office. She told me I wasn't working out in my position, and she had to let me go. I can't say I was surprised - I knew I had been walking on thin ice. But I was still deeply disappointed in myself. I felt like I had let her down, and more than that, I was ashamed. Around that same time, I started falling behind on my mortgage payments.

In March 2014, I had both positive and negative experiences. I landed a job with an electric company. The pay was excellent – comparable to what someone with a degree would earn. And for the first time in a while, my financial situation felt stable. In that same month, Grace gave birth to another beautiful baby girl named Katie. She is a bright spot in all our lives. But personally, I was still struggling. I only lasted five months in my new position. I was terminated the day before my birthday in August 2014.

One night a friend gave me some drugs, and I took them while drinking. The next morning, I woke up with a swollen ankle and bruises on my arms and face. I had fallen on my patio, but I didn't even remember falling - or going to bed. As I struggled to get up that morning, barely able to walk, I asked myself, *what am I doing? How did I end up like this?* It was a wake-up call. I realized I couldn't keep living this way. I needed to make changes – real, lasting changes. And I knew they had to start now.

Chapter 17 – Uncertainty

Proverbs 3:5 "Trust in the Lord with all your heart and lean not on your own understanding."

The end of 2014 and the four years that followed were a time of deep instability in my life. After losing my job, I fell further behind on mortgage payments and was eventually forced to put my home on the market as a short sale. It was December – just two weeks before Christmas - when I found myself packing with no idea where I was going next. I felt like Abraham must have felt when God told him to leave his country and his people and go to a land that He would show him (Genesis 12:1-3). I put all my belongings in storage and waited for God to reveal the next step.

The Lord provided - but in ways I hadn't expected. A friend had a vacant house and graciously offered it to me temporarily until I could find a job and get back on my feet financially. I moved in at the beginning of 2015 and stayed for five months while working a temp job. At the end of May, the owner asked me to leave. Soon after, another friend – whose home was in foreclosure – told me I could stay there as long as I needed. I moved in June, retrieved my things from storage, and thought I'd finally have a place to settle for a while. Around that time, I landed a full-time job at a law firm as a Subpoena Clerk. It paid only half of what I earned in previous positions, but I was deeply grateful for permanent work. It gave me a sense of security and normalcy – something I had been craving for a long time. Then, in October, the owner of the house called to say it had sold. I had to be out by November. I felt helpless. I simply didn't make enough money to afford a place of my own. Doors stayed shut, and for the first time in my walk with the Lord, I felt like He had let me down. Of course, He hadn't. It was just part of His plan for me at that time. I didn't understand what He was doing, but that season brought me to a place of total surrender and trust - and that was exactly what I needed.

My daughter and son-in-law offered to let me stay with them and their three children. It wasn't the ideal situation, but it helped all of us financially. For the third time in two years, I put my belongings back in storage. Grace and Tyler were incredibly gracious – they gave me the master bedroom with my own bathroom, a kindness I didn't take for granted. Around that time, the law firm where I was working moved across the bridge to Pinellas County, which made my daily commute even longer.

Not long after the move, a friend reached out after reading a Facebook post I made. She and her husband came by and surprised me with a check for $2,000. It was an incredibly generous gift, and I was overwhelmed with gratitude that they would do something so kind and selfless. That money could help me get into a place of my own, but I also knew I needed a job that paid enough to support myself. I deposited the check into a savings account and held onto it, waiting and praying for the right opportunity to come.

Another blessing came my way in January when I joined a prison ministry, Hope Rising. We held services twice a month, and I had the opportunity to see the women grow in their relationship with God. It was such a blessing to see the joy they had, as they engaged in worship. We faithfully attended until the ladies were moved to a new facility that was two hours away.

I continued to live with my family and commuting across the bridge for another year. In November 2017, Tyler received a settlement check from an accident he'd been in, and he and Grace planned to buy a home - which meant I had to move once again. A friend told me about a woman who rented rooms, and I reached out. She had one available. I went to see it on a Friday night, just a week before Thanksgiving. It was a four-bedroom mobile home shared by four other women. I gave her a deposit and left in tears. I felt so discouraged - so forgotten by God. Why was I still going through this? Why couldn't I catch a break? Would my life ever feel normal again?

I lived in that home for a year and a half, and it wasn't easy sharing that space with four other women. But, as always, God worked it out for good – just as Romans 8:28 promises. One of my housemates, Nancy, wasn't a believer, and I began praying for her. One day she knocked on my bedroom door and asked me to pray for her because she was having pain in her knee. After I finished praying, she asked, "Would it be too much trouble if you prayed for me every day when you get home from work?" In that moment, I knew God was softening her heart. He was moving in ways I couldn't see.

Another bright spot during that year was the birth of Faith's first baby boy in December. His name is Brady, and he has been an absolute delight to our family. His arrival brought joy and light into a season that had felt so heavy.

In March of 2018, I started a new job at a law firm just five minutes from where I was living. By April, I was finally able to get my own place again. It felt like a step toward stability – but that sense of security was short-lived. In August I lost the job, and my worst fear became a reality. I was living on my own, responsible for all the bills, and suddenly had no income. But even in that difficult time, God was so faithful to me. The first month I was unemployed, someone anonymously paid my rent. The next two months, my rent was covered by a generous friend and my church. Their support reminded me that I wasn't alone – that God was still providing, even when everything felt uncertain. In 2019, I finally got another job. It was steady, and I was grateful. But then the Lord opened a new door – an opportunity that felt like my true calling.

Chapter 18 – Mistakes

Jeremiah 29:11 "For I know the plans I have for you, declares the LORD, plans to prosper you and not to harm you, plans to give you hope and a future."

In 2020, a pandemic swept across the country, and churches everywhere shut their doors. Like many others, I began listening to services online. It was a frightening time for everyone, yet there was also something beautiful about it - people seemed kinder, more thoughtful. We were all in it together, and thankfully we made it through.

That same year, I met a woman with a powerful vision: to open a home for survivors of sex trafficking. We met for lunch one day, and as I shared my story with her, she offered me the position of residential manager once the home was ready. I accepted without hesitation, filled with excitement! I knew I was stepping into my calling – into the purpose for which I was made. We spread the word, searched for the right home, and waited patiently for God to open the door. A full year passed in anticipation.

We found the perfect place, and the timing couldn't have been better. My lease ended on June 30th, and I moved on July 1st. One resident was already living there before I even arrived. It turned out to be one of the hardest moves I've ever made. It poured rain all day, there were issues with the U-Haul truck, and I ended up spending a lot of money hiring someone to help me move. I gave away nearly everything I owned, keeping only my clothes and a few sentimental items and photos.

But after just two weeks, I realized this wasn't the dream I thought it would be. It was nothing like I had imagined - much harder, and very different from what I had hoped. Deep down, I knew I had made a mistake. The truth is, I had seen red flags before I ever moved in, but I ignored them. I was so convinced this was where God wanted me, I didn't let myself consider otherwise. Six weeks in, I made a mistake involving the resident and was dismissed from the ministry. I was given one week to move out, and I had no idea where I was going - much like when I lost my home in 2014. I put my belongings in storage, and with just a small amount of savings and my paycheck, I rented a hotel room for a few days. During this time, I had lost all joy and felt very far from God. I know what I did was wrong, and I had repented. But I still felt forgotten by God. That's when a new door began to open, and He blessed me far above what I could ask for.

Chapter 19 – Changes

Isaiah 43:18-19 "Forget the former things; do not dwell on the past. See, I am doing a new thing! Now it springs up; do you not perceive it? I am making a way in the wilderness and streams in the wasteland."

Faith graciously offered to let me stay with her for as long as I needed. While I was staying there, I heard about a program that helped people with housing. I reached out, had an interview, and soon after, the case manager, Vickie, shared the good news - I qualified. This time, instead of placing me in a shelter, they put me in a hotel and covered the cost. Vickie reassured me not to worry; I could stay there until an apartment became available, though there was a waiting list.

On August 19, 2021, I moved into the hotel, where I would end up staying for five months. Just two days later, I contracted Covid and was sick for a week. I spent my birthday that year sleeping all day. I felt completely isolated – as if I had lost all my friends and was being punished for my past mistakes. But deep down, I knew that was the enemy trying to convince me I was unworthy. This was just another difficult time I had to endure.

Yet in that stillness, something powerful happened. Alone in that hotel room, God began to restore my soul. He did a deep work in my heart. I found peace. I became content with where I was. I had everything I needed, and I was truly grateful. I used that solitude to grow closer to Him, to rebuild relationships I had neglected. Still, something was missing. I felt an aching need to talk to someone about everything I had been through - but I didn't know who to turn to. I was too embarrassed to reach out to any of the pastors at the church I had been attending.

In November, I received a call from a placement agency I had registered with earlier. They had an opening at an electric cooperative. I went to the interview and was hired on the spot. The pay was decent, and honestly, just getting out of the hotel for a few hours each day was a blessing. I didn't even have a permanent address to give. Thankfully, the founder of the ministry I was part of allowed me to use their address until I found a place of my own. I was thrilled to be working again. With no major living expenses, I was able to save most of my paycheck – a small but significant step toward rebuilding my life.

My case manager let me know she was leaving for another position. The next one assigned to me turned out to be a believer in Christ. When he came to my hotel room to help me fill out some paperwork, he prayed with me before he left - a breath of fresh air the Lord had provided.

Christmas Day came, and I found myself completely alone in the hotel. No cards, no gifts, no friends or family. But I wasn't feeling sorry for myself. I had found a sense of contentment, and I was genuinely okay. I bought a honey-baked ham and went over to my friend Nancy's apartment, and we shared Christmas dinner – even though she was sick. I also received sweet text messages from my daughters. In the end, it turned out to be a good day. Not long after, Faith told me she was expecting another baby, due in May 2022.

When January 1, 2022, arrived, I had a deep sense that this was going to be a better year. In February, Faith went into labor unexpectedly, and Donny was born two and a half months early, weighing just three and a half pounds. Surrounded by prayers and support, he grew stronger each day and was finally able to go home once he had gained enough weight. Today, he is a happy and healthy three-year-old.

Chapter 20 – Restoration

Job 42:10 "After Job had prayed for his friends, the LORD restored his fortunes and gave him twice as much as he had before."

A friend told me about one of our former campus pastors who was led by God to start his own church - a mobile church named *The Difference*. I registered on the website to receive updates and event notifications. The first gathering I attended was a Christmas caroling event at a retirement community. Pastor Greg and his wife Felicia welcomed me warmly. Walking through the mobile home park, singing to the elderly, was a touching and memorable experience. From that moment, I knew he was the one I was meant to talk to about my situation.

In January, I attended a pancake breakfast and took the opportunity to ask Pastor Greg if he would be willing to meet with me. Without hesitation, he said yes and told me to reach out with a date and time. We met one afternoon at a coffee shop after I got off work. He bought me a coffee, and I spent the next hour sharing my story. I felt ashamed and defeated, as if I had lost all sense of purpose. Pastor Greg listened with compassion. He encouraged me and suggested that I visit the church's website to listen to the daily meditations. I left the coffee shop feeling lighter, with a small but undeniable glimmer of hope. I began listening to the meditations, and just three days later, I emailed Pastor Greg to share the change already happening in my heart. My joy was returning. I felt a renewed sense of excitement about my future. I had gone from feeling lukewarm to having a fire in my soul once again. This is when my heart began to heal.

Two days after meeting with Pastor Greg, I received a phone call from my case manager - an apartment had become available. After living in a hotel for five months, I was more than ready to have a place of my own again. When I went to see the apartment, I was amazed. It was a fully renovated unit with brand-new stainless-steel appliances. It would be ready for me to move in by February 2nd. I was overwhelmed with gratitude to God for opening this door. I could hardly wait for moving day! The program I was part of covered the deposit, along with rent and electricity for an entire year. God had completely turned my situation around. What the enemy meant for evil, God intended for good. (Genesis 50:20)

On moving day, I was packing the few clothes and boxes I had when I received a call from Pastor Greg. He said he was just checking in to see how I was doing. I told him I was in the middle of packing. He asked if I needed any help or if there was anything he could do for me. I explained that I didn't have much to move, but I would be sleeping on the floor since I didn't have a bed. He took time out of his day to bring me an air mattress. It was such a blessing. I was trusting God to provide everything else I needed, and this act of kindness reminded me that He was already doing just that.

On Tuesday, as I was signing the lease for my new apartment, I received a text from Pastor Greg. Attached were pictures of furniture, and he asked if I would like it for my new place. It was a complete living room set, bedroom set, and a dining table. As I looked at the photos, I cried - tears of pure gratitude. That Friday, a crew showed up with everything: furniture, dishes, food, housewares, toiletries – everything I needed. God had given me more than what I had given away. A few days later, a friend came over to help hang pictures, and when it was all done, my little apartment truly felt like home - adorable, cozy, and filled with peace.

The following year, 2023, when I began paying my own rent, it increased by $210. Even so, I was thankful to have a good job and was able to cover my bills while continuing to sow into various ministries. God had truly restored and provided, just as He promised.

In October, the Lord placed it on my heart to start a women's group. He gave me the letters W.O.W., and I knew it was to be called *Women of Worth*. From the beginning, it was a beautiful success. We met on the third Saturday of each month to share food, fellowship, and encouragement. Different speakers came to pour into the group, and each gathering became a time of growth and healing for all of us. Attendance ranged from 10 to 20 women each month, and for that season, it was truly one of the most enjoyable and fulfilling ministries I had ever been part of. *Women of Worth* lasted for a year. In March 2024, I felt led to let it go. Life got busy, a few meetings had to be canceled, and slowly, interest from the group began to fade. Still, I was deeply grateful for the time we shared. It was a gift for that season, and it served its purpose well.

Chapter 21 – Healed Heart

Philippians 3:13-14 "Brothers and sisters, I do not consider myself yet to have taken hold of it. But one thing I do: Forgetting what is behind and straining toward what is ahead, I press on toward the goal to win the prize for which God has called me heavenward in Christ Jesus."

The year 2023 was definitely a better year all around.

Our prison ministry team was finally able to return to Lowell Correctional Institute, the facility to where the women from Hernando were transferred. During one of our visits, we stopped for dinner on the way. As we sat at our table, a woman approached us, placed an envelope in front of us and said, "God bless your work." Inside the envelope was $150.00. God was already blessing our obedience to return.

On Easter Sunday, our church held a beach baptism, and a woman I mentored was baptized. It was a beautiful blessing to see the joy on her face as she rose from the water.

In May, Grace graduated from Hillsborough Community College with a degree in paralegal studies. I couldn't be prouder of her! She's now pursuing her bachelor's degree, has a great job that allows her to work from home, and has made significant financial progress.

In December, our church held an outreach at a local nursing home, where we went Christmas caroling. We shared love and joy with these precious souls, and some even joined in and sang along with us.

Each year I pray about a word to guide me through the year. For 2024, that word was *favor* - and I truly experienced God's favor throughout. The year began on a difficult note due to family issues, which I've chosen not to write about. Amid the storm, I cried out to God more than once, and He remained with me through it all. Eventually, things settled down, and I found myself facing some important decisions.

My lease expired on January 31, and I didn't want to renew it because the rent was so high. For months, I searched for another apartment, only to find that even a one bedroom was too expensive. Still, I trusted God had a place for me – even if it wasn't what I had in mind. A friend happened to be looking for a roommate, and I sensed that's where the Lord wanted me to be. It was a difficult decision. After several days of wrestling with God, I finally obeyed. I moved in with her in February and stayed for eight months. During that time, I was able to save money for when the next move came. The Lord truly blesses obedience, and our time together proved to be a blessing for both of us. As Proverbs 27:17 says, "As iron sharpens iron, so one person sharpens another."

I had been praying for another car – not just for myself, but with the desire to use it to help others and for Kingdom work. The car I was driving was older and had high mileage, but my heart was set on something that could serve a greater purpose. The Lord honored that prayer. In March, my pastor asked to meet with me, and to my surprise, he presented me with a 2016 Hyundai Elantra in mint condition, with only 80,000 miles. It was truly an answer to prayer - God went above and beyond what I expected. I've been using it to give rides to those in need and for ministry purposes, just as I had hoped.

For Mother's Day in May, Grace blessed me with a trip to Louisiana to visit my sister, whom I hadn't seen in six years. We had a wonderful time together, and the next day we visited the gravesite of my mom, dad, and brother – somewhere Grace had never been to before.

In August, for my birthday, Grace blessed me once again – this time with a weekend trip to the beach. When I arrived at the hotel room, I was surprised to find it beautifully decorated with banners, flowers, and a birthday cake. The next day, we went on a speedboat excursion and watched dolphins play in the water. It was one of the most memorable birthdays I've ever had.

In late September, hurricane Helene came through, and the storm surge caused significant damage to those living in the Big Bend region. Then in October, hurricane Milton made landfall on Florida's west coast. According to news reports, Milton was the strongest tropical cyclone in the world in 2024. I'm grateful for those who were spared and prayed for those who suffered loss of property and vehicles.

After the hurricanes, I began to sense that it was time to move into my own place. I had been on the wait list at two different apartment complexes, and both contacted me with availability. But I declined both offers because I felt God had something better – specifically, something more affordable. I chose to wait, trusting Him, and His favor was truly upon me. I eventually moved into a beautifully renovated condominium unit, with rent that was $300 less than the other places. It even included water, sewer, and trash, which the others did not. The community also has a tennis court, basketball court, workout facility, and an Olympic-sized swimming pool. It's such a blessing to be where I am today, and I give God all the glory!

My purpose in writing this Memoir, is to encourage you with the examples of perseverance and testimonies of God's faithfulness. It is my prayer that hope will be restored to those who feel hopeless. In all the hard times I went through, I still saw the goodness of God in every situation. To my friends who are reading this story, be encouraged and remember God is always with you. Don't give up! Find a group with those who will support you when you are facing difficulties. We are not meant to do life alone.

I am thankful that today I can confidently say my heart is completely healed of past wounds. I'm expecting great things in 2025, that God's favor and grace will continue to be upon me and my family. My word for this year is *abundance*. But it's not for material things or money. It's for the abundant life Jesus promises in John 10:10. And I'm truly experiencing that today. I'm expecting great things in 2025, that God's favor and grace will continue to be upon me and my family. My word for this year is *abundance*. But it's not for material things or money. It's for the abundant life Jesus promises in John 10:10. And I'm truly experiencing that today.

You can connect with me on Facebook as Cyndi Sims

Or

On Instagram as CyndiSims2

www.ingramcontent.com/pod-product-compliance
Lightning Source LLC
Chambersburg PA
CBHW061710120626

46550CB00003B/1165